Civil Procedure in Ecuador

Civil Procedure in Ecuador

Josemaria Bustamante

This book was originally published as a monograph in the International Encyclopaedia of Laws/Civil Procedure.

Founding Editor: Roger Blanpain
General Editor: Frank Hendrickx
Volume Editor: Piet Taelman

Wolters Kluwer

Published by:
Kluwer Law International B.V.
PO Box 316
2400 AH Alphen aan den Rijn
The Netherlands
E-mail: international-sales@wolterskluwer.com
Website: lrus.wolterskluwer.com

Sold and distributed in North, Central and South America by:
Wolters Kluwer Legal & Regulatory U.S.
7201 McKinney Circle
Frederick, MD 21704
United States of America
Email: customer.service@wolterskluwer.com

Sold and distributed in all other countries by:
Air Business Subscriptions
Rockwood House
Haywards Heath
West Sussex
RH16 3DH
United Kingdom
Email: international-customerservice@wolterskluwer.com

ISBN 978-94-035-2663-8

e-Book: ISBN 978-94-035-2664-5
web-PDF: ISBN 978-94-035-2665-2

The Author

Josemaria Bustamante has assisted international clients in Multilateral transactions; Cross-border transactions; M&A and Antitrust; Project Financing; Public Procurement; Tax Law; Commercial Law; Corporate Law; International Trade; Arbitration and Litigation in the following sectors: Insurance; Banking & Finance; Commerce; Communications and Telecommunications; Energy; Agrochemical industry; and Food industry. Dr. Bustamante is also avid in Mediation, Arbitration, and Civil litigation. Pro bono work includes having obtained the first certificate of protection in Ecuador and the first patent conferred to a Luthier in Ecuador, which were granted to Luthier Hugo Chiliquinga; Fundación Zaldumbide-Rosales (promoting musicians worldwide); The Global Foodbanking Network, and several individuals, domestic and alien, requiring litigious assistance in Ecuador.

He is a member of the Pichincha Bar Association and an active member in the International Bar Association, the American Bar Association, the Quito Chamber of Commerce, London Chamber of Commerce, and Paris Chamber of Commerce, the Bomchil Group (an association of Latin American Law Firms), and World Services Group. He has also been a Speaker of the American and Washington State Bar Associations, the San Francisco Bar Association, the London Chamber of Commerce, and the Paris Chamber of Commerce. He is also a keen contributor to the International Encyclopedia of Laws.

In 1997, Dr. Bustamante obtained a Licentiate in Juridical Sciences degree and obtained a Republican Courts Barrister degree from Pontificia Universidad Católica del Ecuador. In 2004, he also obtained a Doctorate in Jurisprudence. He is fluent in Spanish and English.

The Author

Table of Contents

Table of Contents

List of Abbreviations

COGEP	General Organic Code of Civil Procedures
COIP	Criminal Code
SENESCYT	High Education, Science, Technology, and Innovation Secretary

List of Abbreviations

General Introduction

§1. General Background (Information on the Political and Legal System of the Country)

1. The Republic of Ecuador is on the Equator (hence its name) and is in the pacific rim of South America. Ecuador obtained its independence in 1830. The territory of Ecuador prior to 1830 was part of a larger country emancipated from the Spanish Empire named Colombia. The territories forming Colombia were the territories basically conforming the Viceroyalty of Santa Fe, which now are those part of Panama, Venezuela, Colombia, and Ecuador. Then Colombia was divided into three Republics: the Bolivarian Republic of Venezuela, the Republic of Colombia (now Colombia and Panama) and the Republic of Ecuador. Eventually, for referential purposes, initial Colombia is now referred to as La Gran Colombia (the Grand Colombia) to differentiate it from the current Republic of Colombia.

With that said, it is of no surprise that the initial legislation applicable in the territories of Ecuador was the legislation initially adopted by Colombia from Spain, and then such legislation adopted by Ecuador from Colombia.

§2. Delimitation of the Subject Matter

I. Definition of the Term "Civil Procedure"

2. There is no legal definition for encompassing the term "civil procedure," but it can basically be framed into any procedure before the judiciary that is neither criminal nor constitutional.

II. Distinction with Other Types of Procedure (Administrative, Criminal)

3. Administrative proceedings are also considered part of civil procedure universe; as administrative proceedings are initiated by a simple application filed into a government agency, such an application is handled at an administrative level within the corresponding government agencies. This would include any application filed within the judicial system venue while remaining at an administrative level. When the application is challenged, rejected, observed, or opposed, it becomes a quarrelsome proceeding whose genesis is the original application. These proceedings are governed by the Administrative Code of 2017, and the Proceedings Act of

2018. When the administrative proceeding has come to an end, meaning all administrative recourses or appeals have been exhausted, and the highest level of authority has finally denied the application with no avail, or there is, at any administrative stage, the applicant's willingness to move the proceeding upward to judiciary level, the administrative proceeding can be appealed before the Court of Administrative Appeals, the process of which shall be governed by the General Organic Code of Civil Procedures (COGEP) as well.

Criminal proceedings are such proceedings that are required to solve a criminal case, and constitutional proceedings are such that are required to solve Constitutional issues, both of which are handled by their own set of rules. However, COGEP is an alternative law for all sorts of processes and proceedings when there is silence on the other laws for a given matter.

III. Are There Separate Court Systems and Rules of Procedure?

4. Before getting into the jurisdictional systems, I would like to mention that the Constitution of 1998 granted nationality to all those indigenous communities claiming to possess their own nationality (based on cultural, socio-economic, and ancestral principles), eradicating the concept of "Ecuadorian nationality" and replacing it by granting all Ecuadorians (indigenous or else) the Ecuadorian citizenship, based on the argument that citizenship was a modern concept overriding the concept of nationality. Moreover, it provides that when any law or international treaty refers to "nationality," it should be read as if referring to "citizenship." With that said, the Constitution granted indigenous communicates their own capacity to rule and make justice on their own, but just within the boundaries of their own communities (including outsiders meddling with their community). Indigenous communities do not have a judicial system or judiciary, per se. It is not well-organized or systematic. The proceeding is accommodated on a day-to-day basis, making circumstantial justice based on their own beliefs. Their ignorance on basic legal terms, some of them subtracted from modern societies, yet some others influenced by more sophisticated leaders but equally uneducated, have turned their so-called justice into excesses, such as the sentencing of alleged criminals (without due process that is) to be immolated on *in fraganti* crimes, without formal due process, following the accusation of so-called trustworthy witnesses.

Current Constitution, in effect since 2008, once again grants all Ecuadorians the Ecuadorian nationality; yet, still maintaining the rights of the indigenous nationalities to do justice by their own hand, providing in its § 167 that the capacity to make justice is given by the people, and it is exercised by the different bodies of the Judicial System and by other figures and agencies established by the Constitution; and in its § 171 that the officers in chief from the communities, people, and indigenous nationalities shall exercise jurisdictional powers, based on their ancestral traditions, and their own law, within their territory, guaranteeing the participation of women in the decision-making. The officers in chief shall apply their own norms and proceedings for the solutions of their internal conflicts that are not against the Constitution human rights duly recognized in international treaties. The State warrants that the indigenous justice rulings be respected by every and all government agencies and

State institutions. The mechanisms of coordination and cooperation between indigenous justice and ordinary justice can and must be regulated by Congress acts.

Accordingly, there would be two very different systems: (i) one that is well identified, regulated, and academically procedural: The Ordinary Judicial System; and (ii) another one exposed to the criteria of every indigenous community in their different forms: the Indigenous Judicial System. The Ordinary Judicial System, then, is a single system, with separate stages. The Ordinary Judicial System is composed of: (i) the National Court of Justice, the highest recursive court (current equivalent to a Supreme Court or *Cour de Cassation*); (ii) the Provincial Court of Justice, the highest appellate court in every province (current equivalent to a Superior Court); (iii) the first instance courts established by law; and (iv) the courts of peace. The Judiciary Council is the body in charge of administering, governing, surveilling, and disciplining the Ordinary Judicial System. Public Notaries, judicial auctioneers, judicial depositaries, and other officers as stablished by the law are ancillary judicial officers.

Arbitration is also recognized and regulated; and there is the Constitutional Court, which is an independent court, free from any meddling or intervention by any other State institution.

In addition, prior to current COGEP, the Armed Forces and the National Police Department were subject to their own courts. Nowadays, both are subject to the same Ordinary Judicial System.

§3. Sources of Civil Procedure Law (Including a Brief Historical Perspective)

5. Then, since the creation of the Republic of Ecuador, this country started enacting its own laws (or, better said, copying laws duly enacted in other countries). The Chilean Civil Code structured by the Venezuelan Andrés Bello (based on the Napoleonic Code) was passed into law in 1857 and promulgated in 1860. At about the same time, the Code of Commerce was enacted emulating the Spanish Code of Commerce. A couple more Civil Codes were enacted in 1930 and 1970; yet, keeping some aberrant errors until the latest amendments to the Code. The Commercial Code suffered a similar fate with evident anachronisms (even worse than with respect to the Civil Code), having been reenacted by the National Assembly (local current equivalent to a Congress) in 2019.

The first collection of civil procedures laws that I have been able to put my hands on is the Code of Civil Judgments of 1917 with further Codes of Civil Procedures enacted in 1953, 1987, 2005. While drafting this monograph, the applicable piece of legislation is COGEP of 2015 (fully applicable since 2016). The latter changed the rules of civil procedures that the country was accustomed to since dawn, an anachronic piece of legislation that had endured for almost two centuries, forcing the system to be deceived, and forcing the proceeding to last as long as thirty-four years (record time). The Code of Civil Judgments regulated the following written proceedings: (i) the Ordinary Procedure, which was defined as such in which all formalities and solemnities were to be in place; and (ii) the Summary Procedure, defined as such in which some of such formalities may be skipped, and the terms were briefer. Accordingly, every process having no special procedural rules was to be handled through the Ordinary Procedure. Such proceedings were classified into lower-amount processes and higher-amount processes (such in excess of Four Hundred Sucres, currently USD 62,500). Then there was the Executive Process, which, in addition to serving for executing all rulings (domestic or foreign) obtained from other processes, it served to execute executive titles (i.e., securities), such as affidavits sworn before a competent judge, the first certified copy of public deeds, private documents judicially acknowledged, letters of exchange or promissory notes, wills and judicial auctions, undertaking or transactional minutes. Then, there was the verbal-summary process, applicable to all cases that were to be known in an oral manner and swift fashion, such as damages, but, did not establish which cases, exactly, were to be known in an oral manner and swift fashion. Within ten days after the claim was verbally filed, the judge would call for a preliminary hearing; if there was evidence to be submitted, the judge would grant a six days evidentiary term, after which the judge would issue his ruling within the next three days. These proceedings were solved in a matter of weeks. Such utopia may have lasted for the first half of the last century. Then there were several special processes, such as: (i) the proceeding to grant a license to a married woman that required to execute a contract or appear in court when the husband unreasonably denied such license (such license requirements are now obsolete and abrogated); (ii) alimony, and other proceedings.

The Code of Civil Judgments of 1917 encompassed three instances: (i) the first instance; (ii) the appellation before the Superior Court; and (iii) the third instance before the Supreme Court (there was no notion of Cassation at the time). Hence, virtually every single lawsuit underwent such three instances, eventually jamming the courts.

The classification of the proceedings by the Code of Civil Judgments into an ordinary, verbal summary, executive and special proceedings has been maintained, with minor variations, ever since. The Cassation Act abrogated the third instance before the Supreme Court making proceedings handled at the Supreme Court as a separate case; therefore, not every case is entitled to cassation. About 75% of the cases are denied cassation. Current COGEP abrogated the Cassation Act providing its own rules of cassation. The verbal-summary proceeding, which was supposed to be an oral and expeditious proceeding (hence the name) was neither verbal nor expeditious. In fact, I personally successfully handled a multimillion verbal-summary case defending a client that lasted more than twelve years, as it endured challenging the judges, appointing deputy judges and two cassation recourses. It was neither verbal nor summary.

§4. General Features of the Administration of Justice in Civil Matters

I. Characteristics of the Procedure: Adversary and/or Inquisitorial Procedure, Role of the Judge and of the Parties, Oral and/or Written Procedure

6. The idea for the enactment of COGEP seems to be to favor verbalization and to expedite the procedures as much as possible. The claim is submitted in a fully written document demanding the administration of justice; then, after reviewing the writ of claim, the judge has the following options:

(i) § 146 the judge may request the completion or clarification of the claim (this initial judicial motion can be subject of appeal or even cassation); or,
(ii) § 147 the judge may reject the claim due to the following reasons:
   (a) inappropriate joint (accumulation of) actions; or,
   (b) lack of jurisdiction. When the judge considers he/she has no jurisdiction over the matter of the litis, due to venue, matter, etc.[1]

Then, following the judge's request to complete or clarify the claim, having the plaintiff completed or clarified its claim, the process should continue its due course of action. The plaintiff is entitled to file an appeal against the judge's request to complete and clarify; in which case, provided there is a higher-level resolution (appellate court or cassation court) to continue the process, it should continue its due course of action without additional completion or clarification.

Finally, when the court has indefectibly accepted the claim overcoming any of the abovementioned alternatives, the court shall call for the first hearing in which the defendant must submit its defense orally (and also in writing) and submit a counterclaim if any, in which case, the court shall grant the plaintiff the right to announce new evidence (if the defendant has contributed with new arguments to be proved) and additional time for the plaintiff to submit answers to the counterclaim. At all times, the court will endeavor the parties to settle, in such a way that the court is even entitled to send the process to a mediation center. Should there be no settlement after the mediation proceeding, the process shall return to court for its continuation.

All evidence must be announced in advance, and the parts must have access to all evidence before submitting their answers. The court is able and encouraged by law to manage the proceeding, inquire, and to promote the parties into acting.

1. This judges' prerogative to reject claims on their free will is a new tool based on Constitutional provisions (§ 76), which allow judges to reject many claims based on lack of jurisdiction, and so easing their load of work, even though being fully competent indeed.

II. Fundamental Guarantees (Constitution, Human Rights Treaties, General Principles of the Law): Establishment of Courts by Law, Independence and Impartiality, Reasons, Publicity, Fair Trial, Reasonable Time, Appeal, Etc.

7. The Constitution is the highest norm establishing all the rights and principles of the Ecuadorian community, and the structure of the Ecuadorian State. According to § 424 of the Constitution, this is the highest norm and prevails over any other provision in the Ecuadorian legal system. That means that all validly enacted International Treaties or Conventions are to be preferred over any legal provision enacted by Congress. Pursuant to § 424, below the Constitution, are the International Treaties the Congress Acts (organic and non-organic), Ordinances, Executive Decrees, Regulations, and so on and so forth. In principle, the Courts are not allowed to "create" law or to reject a legal provision favoring a "better" right or legal principle. However, § 424 of the Constitution also provides that this and the International Treaties of human rights granting higher rights to those established in the Constitution, prevail over any other legal provision or State's Act. The latter has prompted some international law activists to argue that such Human Rights Treaties have the highest hierarchy, even above the Constitution itself. The Ecuadorian Courts are only allowed to construe the meaning of certain obscured legal provisions, but they are not allowed to alter the meaning of the law, or to amend a legal provision arguing interpretation of the law or the applicability of a better right.

§ 180 of the Judicial Branch Organic Code provides that in case of obscurity or doubt on the application of the law, the National Court is entitled to issue general and compulsory Resolution that must be obeyed by all until the National Assembly provides otherwise, if ever. However, the Ecuadorian Courts in their eagerness to create law have taken further steps by interpreting its meaning. One clear example is a recent case in which even though the Constitution expressly provides the following:

> § 67. Family is conceived in its diverse types. The State shall protect it as a fundamental core of the society and shall guarantee the conditions integrally favoring the attainment of its purpose. These shall be constituted through juridical or factual links and shall be based in the equality of rights and opportunity of its members.
> Matrimony is the union of a man and a woman, *shall* be founded in the free will of the engaging parties and in the equality of their rights, obligations and legal capacity.

The Constitutional Court has construed that such Constitutional provision, accepted by referendum in 2008 by an overwhelming majority, is not in tune with the rest of the Constitutional provisions, the international principles and human rights, and order the Civil Registry to register same sex matrimony. Hence, nowadays the Ecuadorian courts do not seem willing to allow the laws to follow their fate, or to respect the other powers or duties; they prefer to make amends on their own, according to their better judgement. This clear meddling of the judiciary into the powers of other bodies is the first reminiscence of common law that we have seen in Ecuador.

Part I. Judicial Organization

Chapter 1. The Courts and Their Members

§1. COURTS

I. Structure of the Court System

8. Pursuant to the Constitution of 2008, § 167, the power to serve justice is vested in the people and implemented through the Judicial System and other bodies and powers as established by the Law (Article 38 of the Judicial Branch Organic Code), to wit: (i) the National Court (current local equivalent to a Supreme Court) with its corresponding Co-Justices; (ii) the Provincial Courts (current local equivalent to a Superior Court) with its corresponding Co-Justices; (iii) the First Instance Judges with their corresponding jurisdictions as established by the law; (iv) the Peace Courts; and (v) alternative means of serving justice, such as Arbitration.

Other ancillary bodies of the Judicial System are the Notaries, the judicial auctioneers, the judicial depositaries, and others as established by the law.

The Ombudsman, the General Attorney, and the General Prosecutor are autonomous bodies of the Judicial System.

The chiefs from the diverse indigenous communities and nationalities existing in Ecuador, according to § 171, have an inalienable right to establish their own judicial system and implement their own justice within their people and territories, according to their ancestral traditions and personal due process. The chiefs shall apply their own norms and processes for the solution of their internal affairs and conflicts, provided such application of justice does not interfere with the Constitution and internationally accepted human rights. The State shall warrant that the judicial decisions from such communities be respected by all government institutions and agencies. Such decisions are subject to constitutional surveillance, and the law is to establish the mechanisms of coordination and cooperation between the indigenous and ordinary justice systems.

Such entitlements vested in the indigenous communities have served the purpose of abusing of power and violation of the law.

II. Administration of the Court

9. One can make a career in the judicial system, which regulates the internship, capacitation, education, promotion, stability, evaluation, disciplinary regime, and seniority in the Judicial Branch System (§ 35 of the Judicial Branch Organic Code).

New members of the Judicial System are elected through public contests. In the election of a new member and the promotion of existing members, the principles of equity, probity, no discrimination, publicity, opposition and merits are to be considered. Individuals may be elected on a permanent or a temporary basis. Public servants of the Judicial System are classified as follows: (i) all judges are considered within the jurisdictional system; (ii) all other servants are considered administrative personnel of the Judicial System; (iii) prosecutors belong to the Prosecution System; (iv) all other servants belong to the administrative system of the General Prosecution System; (v) the Ombudsmen belong to attorneys career within such entity; and (vi) any other individual serving for the Ombudsman System belong to such system as administrative personnel. The judges, general prosecutors, and ombudsmen are governed by the Judicial Branch Organic Code, and the administrative personnel are governed by the Civic Service and Administrative Career Organic Act. The latter are banned from acting as judges, prosecutors or ombudsmen, even by way of substitution, delegation, as alternates, or temporary.

In the Judicial System, once a claim is submitted, the claims, along with all their attachments, are classified and registered electronically (the barristers can even receive all sorts of notifications by e-mail, and see the progress of their cases through the Judiciary Council's Web Page). Then, the claim is allotted to the corresponding judge through balloting.

The Court had historically been given recess (called "vacancy"). The Congress decided not to allow the Judicial system to be paralyzed at any time and withdrew Courts Vacancy. In 2013, the Code was once again amended to provide that servants of the Judicial System shall be entitled to an annual thirty days leave of absence after eleven months of continuous servitude, which can be accumulated up to sixty days. The vacancy calendar shall be approved by the Judiciary Council, and the latter entity approved the calendar on January 3, 2020.

Hence, as of January 3, 2020, the Courts are once again entitled to Vacancy from December 23 through January 6 according to the following schedule:

- in the Sierra (The Highlands) and the Amazonia (Oriental Lowlands) from August 1 to August 15; and
- in the Coast (Occidental Lowlands) and Insular Region (Galápagos Islands), from March 17 to March 31.

The Judiciary Council is the government, administrative, surveillance, and discipline body of the Judicial System.

III. Bench and "Ministère Public"/Public Prosecutor (If Any)

10. The General Prosecutor, as per § 411 of the Criminal Code (COIP), is the entity in charge of filing public accusations or indictments against a presumed offender of criminal laws. Any individual can report to the General Prosecutor the commitment of a crime, but only the General Prosecutor is entitled to file an indictment to the Courts.

On the other hand, the General Attorney, as per § 2 of the General Attorney Act, is the one in charge of defending the State's interests; it is the State's judicial legal representative. The courts are required to summon the General Attorney in every case in which the State's interests are involved. In addition, the General Attorney is allowed to reply to consultations submitted by any and all government agencies whose interpretation of the law is compulsory on the government agency that has submitted the consultation, but it is not generally mandatory, not even against the citizens involved in the consultation. Pursuant to § 4 of the Arbitration Act, after a conflict has arisen, arbitration is applicable against government agencies, provided there is prior clearance from the General Attorney.

IV. Appointment of Judges (Public Prosecutors and of Members of the "Ministère Public")

11. The Judiciary Council (§ 258 of the Judicial Branch Organic Code) is formed by five members that are elected by the Council of Citizens Participation and Social Control from lists of three individuals chosen by the President of the National Court, the General Prosecutor, the Ombudsman, the President of the Republic, and the National Assembly, through public inquisition and surveillance and public challenging.

The Justices and Co-Justices of the Supreme Court are elected by the Judiciary Council through a proceeding of merits, opposition, challenge and social control. The parity of men and women is favored.

The Judiciary Council also appoints and evaluates the Justices and Co-Justices of the Provincial Courts, the First Instance Judges, District Prosecutors, and other members of the Judicial System.

The Court of Peace Justices are elected by the members of the different communities through a process implemented by the Judiciary Council; however, being submitted to the Court of Peace or to Arbitration is optional.

§2. Members of the Judiciary

12. The members of the Judiciary must be duly certified and admitted as Ecuadorian lawyers with a solid academic career, ethically irreproachable. Those with master's degrees and even PhD degrees shall be preferred.

I. Incompatibilities (§§ 77–79 of the Judicial Branch Organic Code)

13. Pursuant to §§ 77–79 of the Judicial Branch Organic Code, the judicial personnel are considered incompatible if they fall into the following categories:

(1) those under judicial interdiction (appointed guardian), even such having performed assignment of goods, or to whom a creditors' preference or bankruptcy proceedings have been initiated (while not rehabilitated);
(2) those sentenced to imprisonment while serving time; in case of imprisonment rulings due to extortion, bribery, racketeering, or embezzlement, government fraud, or prevarication, the inability will be permanent;
(3) those being prosecuted for crimes considering prison or reclusion, under final judicial notice, while the notice is valid;
(4) those whose free exercise of their legal profession has been suspended;
(5) anyone employed by any government agency, or been a public server by public election (except university professors, who can exercise after judiciary working hours);
(6) those sanctioned with disciplinary sanction with destitution or termination of office;
(7) the ministers of any cult while exercising the ministry;
(8) those being incompatible to form a part of any government agency;
(9) those having goods or funds in tax heavens; and
(10) the spouse, concubine, or relative to the appointing authority or any of its members, or any other employee or dignitary of the judiciary.

II. End of Functions

14. The functions of a judge can be terminated in the following cases:

(1) permanent impairment, when the judge is permanently impaired from acting as a judge (i.e., Parkinson's disease, Alzheimer's disease, senility, or inability to control his/her thoughts);
(2) death;
(3) resignation (when the judge has rendered his voluntary and irrevocable notice of resignation); or
(4) destitution (when the judge has been terminated by the Judiciary Council for disciplinary violations).

III. Discipline

15. Pursuant to §§ 107–109 of the Judicial Branch Organic Code, the Judicial personnel is personally liable for the following violations:

(1) Light Violation, corresponding to a written call of attention or a pecuniary sanction of no more than 10% of his/her stipend (according to the discretional authority of the person in charge of sanctioning):

(a) Three or more tardy passes, provided they do not exceed more than five a month, or three abandonment of duties in working hours.

(b) To meet with one of the parties or its defendant for dealing with matters concerning a case without summoning the other party.

(c) To perform activities that are not related to his/her judicial duties.

(d) To verbally or in writing harm or abuse his/her fellow servants or the users of the judicial system. If the abuse is considered a felony, it shall be prosecuted according to COIP.

(e) To refrain from acting or acting late with no justification.

(f) To refrain from rendering the information to which is bound to deliver.

(g) To use the working station or court for activity other than judicial activity.

(h) To perform purchase and sale activities within the judicial institution premises.

(i) To damage the goods of the judicial institution.

(j) When a claim against the judge in charge of a case (*recusación*) has been accepted due to unjustified retardation in delivering.

Three reiterative light sanctions within a one-year term shall be the cause of suspension.

(2) Serious Violation, corresponding to a cause of suspension of no more than thirty days:

(a) Verbal or written aggressions should the epithets be considered serious.

(b) Showing up to work in drunken conditions or under the effects of psychotropic or stupefacient substances, or consuming alcoholic, psychotropic or stupefacient substances at work.

(c) Propitiating, organizing, or being an activist in the halting of the justice system service.

(d) Causing serious damage to goods, equipment, documents, files, that may be under his/her custody, maintenance, or use, due to negligence, willful disregard of duties.

(e) Committing twice the omission of delivering the information that is bound to deliver.

(f) Rejecting willingly to sign the minutes, official notices, and judicial proceedings.

(g) Allowing preventive incarceration to expire.

(h) Not grounding his/her acts, decision, resolutions, rulings, well enough; or violate the constitutional rights set forth in §§ 75, 76 and 77.

(i) Not notifying on time.

Committing these faults reiteratively for three occasions in a consecutive year shall be the cause of destitution.

(3) Very Serious Violations, subject to destitution:

(a) vulnerating, under the excuse of supervising the service, the internal independence of the public servants of the Judicial System;

(b) leaving the place of work for more than three consecutive working days or for more than five nonconsecutive working days in a single month;

(c) having been sanctioned with pecuniary sanction for more than three times in the lapse of one year;
(d) unlawfully retaining documents, processes, or goods of the Judiciary Branch or third parties that are on his/her desk or office;
(e) introducing documents to the process extemporaneously or substituting them, or mutilating the processes;
(f) exercising the legal profession, directly or through a third person;
(g) participating in the proceedings that he/she is to be part as a judge, prosecutor or ombudsman;
(h) having received a condemnation subject to the incarceration of more than six months as author, or accomplice for a willful crime or any crime against women or the family members;
(i) providing false information or use fabricated documents for the selection, opposition contest, and registration of his/her appointment;
(j) sexual harassment;
(k) soliciting or receiving loans, favors, services putting in doubt the public servant's impartiality;
(l) manipulating the Judicial System's informatic system;
(m) manipulating the causes' balloting;
(n) revealing the content of a position submitted through a close envelope extemporaneously;
(o) not collecting or appropriating the notarial fees without due consideration, or charge more than provided by the law;
(p) revealing information over investigative acts that due to its nature they can favor or prejudice any party illegitimately;
(q) abstaining from appearing to an audience, except for force majeure, or Acts of God; and
(r) lack of serving process to the persons that are being investigated or processed.

The Judiciary Council is in charge of reviewing any disciplinary action and imposing sanctions.

Chapter 2. The Bar

16. The bar consisted of being accepted by any collegiate lawyers' organization called "*Colegio de Abogados.*" Nowadays, such requirement no longer exists, and all lawyers are free to exercise their profession at will. However, in order to work as a barrister, a license with the Judiciary System must be obtained.

§1. Exercise of the Legal Profession

I. Conditions for Admission

17. An Ecuadorian or foreign college degree duly validated or homologated by the High Education, Science, Technology, and Innovation Secretary (SENESCYT) is required to exercise the legal profession. For representing litigants at court (*litigation attorney at law* or barrister), in addition to the above validation, the lawyers must register their college degree at the judiciary and obtain their registration number. Only those with judiciary registration number can enter the judiciary facilities.

Any person may be represented at court through a judicial prosecutor or barrister. Pursuant to the Lawyers Act, though, when a power of attorney has been granted in Ecuador, the judicial prosecutor must be a duly registered, licensed, and admitted attorney at law, and the powers must be granted through a public deed with the solemnities incorporated by a Notary Public; on the other hand, when a power of attorney has been granted abroad, none of the mentioned requirements is applicable, but the judicial prosecutor must act through a duly admitted barrister.

II. Rights and Duties

18. Lawyers with college degrees duly validated by SENESCYT are allowed to exercise their legal profession and even be appointed notaries, and other judiciary positions, but only those having obtained a judiciary registration are allowed to participate in court judiciary prosecutors or barristers.

III. Discipline

19. Pursuant to § 337 of the Judicial Branch Organic Act, the following lawyers shall be suspended for a maximum term of three months from their professional exercise:

(1) those condemned to incarceration while serving time;
(2) when the lawyers neglect from providing explanations to their mandates or clients, without reasonable excuse;
(3) when, in any way, it is evidenced that the lawyers have been appropriated, malversation, fraud, or wrongly used funds in detriment of their clients, disregarding the civil and criminal responsibilities;

(4) when letting banned individuals litigate through him/her;
(5) reiterative injuria; and
(6) when the lawyer fails to appear at a hearing when his/her presence is necessary unless there is force majeure or Acts of Gods preventing the appearance.

The judiciary Council oversees the imposition of disciplinary sanctions up to the destitution of profession.

§2. (Public) Institutions and (Private) Organizations

20. The lawyers' association (Colegio de Abogados) used to be a private institution formed by all lawyers in charge of disciplinary sanctions; now, it is only a group of lawyers who promote the legal profession. Everything else is overseen by the Judiciary Council.

Chapter 3. The Bailiffs

21. Since there are so many definitions of a bailiff throughout the world, we are just going to limit our definition to the person in charge of servicing the legal process, and some duties of noticing other legal documents.

According to § 53 of COGEP, a summons is an act by which a defendant is informed about the tenor of a claim or petition of a preliminary proceeding that has been initiated against that person and the motions that affect them. It is intriguing to see how the definition implies that the defendant is to know the tenor of the claim, and later on, the same Code provides for other means for serving process where the defendant neither knows the tenor of the claim nor the fact that a claim has been initiated. Anyhow, the definition should just provide as the act by which it is being known that a defendant is entitled to appear in court to answer a suit which has been initiated against the defendant.

Anyhow, whatever its concept, a proper summons is an essential element of the process, without which the process is void and null, and should be considered so from the stage in which there has been lack of summons, provided lack of summons has disrobed the defendant's right of defense.

§1. Exercise of the Profession

22. Bailiffs are basically judicial officers from the Bailiff Office in charge of serving the defendants process, by handing them in person the writ of claim and further motions affecting the claim to the defendant.

§2. (Public) Institutions and (Private) Organizations

23. As regulated by the Judiciary Council, there are bailiffs accredited in Quito and Guayaquil and other main jurisdictions established by the National Court. For that, there are Bailiff Offices surveilled and controlled by the Provincial Courts.

In addition, the Judiciary Council may verify due compliance by natural or moral persons with the legal requirements to act as private bailiffs and validate them. The process of verifying and validating private bailiffs is through a public precontract proceeding.

Either public or private, both serve the court and not private interests. In other words, the proceeding of the servicing process is a public proceeding; the private bailiffs would be serving the courts. In fact, plaintiffs are not allowed to have any contact with the bailiff.

Part II. Jurisdiction

Chapter 1. Domestic Jurisdiction

24. Pursuant to § 15 of the Civil Code, all goods located in Ecuador are governed by Ecuadorian laws. Therefore, it is easy to imply that all real estate property located in Ecuadorian territory, including premises property of foreign states (for example, consulates and embassies), are governed by Ecuadorian laws. Goods may be tangible and intangible; accordingly, all tangibles and intangibles located in Ecuador are governed by Ecuadorian law; therefore, all rights (being intangibles) located in Ecuador are governed by Ecuadorian law. But, how can one know where an intangible, such as a right, is located? Will it be based on the individual who holds the right, or will it be based on the tangible in which the right is expressed? The latter is a matter entirely subject to Conflicts of Law or International Private Law.

Following the same pattern, all goods located in Ecuador are also subject to Ecuadorian jurisdiction. Following the provisions of the Commercial Code, contracts executed abroad may be subject to a foreign jurisdiction; yet, contracts signed in Ecuador should be subject to Ecuadorian jurisdiction unless, of course, is otherwise expressed in the contract (if mercantile or commercial).

Former Code of Civil Procedures established that in order for foreign judgments to be executed in Ecuador, the foreign process in its entirety was to be scrutinized by Ecuadorian Courts so that such foreign judgments would not violate any Ecuadorian provisions of public order, being there no concept to "provisions of public order." Now, COGEP is silent with respect to scrutinizing compliance with Ecuadorian provisions of public order. Therefore, provided the foreign judgment complies with the formalities required on its country of origin, including apostille, it is subject to execution in Ecuador.

The exequatur, of course, must be considered under the light of reciprocity. Accordingly, foreign judgments coming from countries in which Ecuadorian judgments are being executed should be equally executed in Ecuador. On the contrary, judgments from countries where Ecuadorian judgments fail to be executed, where reviewing the merits of the Ecuadorian process is due, might not be executed in Ecuador either.

§1. SUBJECT MATTER JURISDICTION

25. Under COGEP, subject matter jurisdiction is basically divided into administrative matters: taxation; civil and commercial actions; labor; family: and juvenile.

I. Factors to Be Taken into Account (E.g., the Value of the Claim, Other Factors)

26. An initial factor to be considered is the value of the claim. There is one proceeding applicable for collections, the monetary value of which is lower than fifty minimum wages (currently about USD 20,000) called "Monitorio" proceeding, § 356 COGEP. It is consensual that it is a monetary collection proceeding intended to be the swiftest of them all.

II. Main Claims and Ancillary Claims

27. A main claim is the only possible claim; no alternative or subsidiary claims are allowed. However, an accumulation of claims or filing several claims in the same brief is allowed. Even though the law does not expressly provide for the feasibility of accumulating claims, it does provide that the judge can reject a writ of claim, or the defendant can validly file an answer rejecting the claims should there be an improper accumulation of claims; therefore, implying that an accumulation of claims is feasible. In fact, the judge can only reject a claim for lack of subject matter jurisdiction and improper accumulation of claims. As per § 15 COGEP, in order to file a proper accumulation of claims, the following must be considered:

(i) Identic persons and goods, even if the claims are different.
(ii) Identic persons and claims, even when the goods are different.
(iii) Identic claims and things, even when the persons are different.
(iv) When the claims emanate from the same cause, even when the persons, the goods, and the claims are different.
(v) When the matter of the litis is comprised of a gender being the matter of another process.

Ancillary claims are limited to interests, costs, expenses, and limited lawyer's fees.

On the other hand, counterclaims are accepted basically against all claims, § 154 COGEP, unless expressly excluded.

III. Overview of the Jurisdiction of the Different Courts

28.

(a) Pursuant to the law, there is to be a Family Judge in every County (Canton), who is to decide over the following issues:
    (1) Any marital situation established by the Civil Code, including the appointment and removal of legal guardians, and inheritance.
    (2) Any concubinage matters or factual unions.
    (3) In some cases, women violence, but not femicides.
    (4) Everything related to the rights and entitlements of children and adolescents.
(b) The law also provides that in each District, there have to be as many Labor Judges as established by the Judiciary Council, whose territorial jurisdiction may comprise the whole District or just part of it. These Labor Judges shall decide on individual employment conflicts not entrusted to the decision of any other authority.
(c) Likewise, in every District, there must be the number of Civil and Commercial Judges as established by the Judiciary Council. These judges shall decide on the following issues:
    (1) every voluntary jurisdiction issue not entrusted to any other authority;
    (2) every issue regarding patrimony, assets, equity, or property, not entrusted to any other authority;
    (3) all claims for losses and damages, including those derived from criminal actions when in the criminal process there has been no particular claim (*querella*);
    (4) any collusion claim; and
    (5) other established by the law.

The National Court is competent to know any admissible cassation recourse, and its venues are classified into the following subject matters:

(a) Administrative Matters:
    (i) such originated from lawsuits filed against administrative rulings drafted down at an Administrative Venue of the Provincial Courts (every case is initiated from a petition submitted at a government agency, including industrial property);
    (ii) lawsuits originated from Contracts or agreements executed by the State or any government agency and the private sector;
    (iii) lawsuits initiated by the private sector for inactivity or deficiency in the services rendered by the State or public sector, and its diverse government agencies, and the private sector in charge of rendering public services, including actions for losses and damages;
    (iv) conflicts of competence among the agencies of the public sector; and
    (v) others, as established by the law.
(b) Taxation:

(i) Such originated from lawsuits filed against administrative rulings drafted down at a Tax Venue of the Provincial Courts, including customs.
(ii) Any actions submitted to challenge State Regulations, City Hall Ordinances, Resolutions, Decrees, and any other general norms containing tax provisions that are not considered a Congress Act.

(c) Criminal (including police and military force proceedings), and transit matters.
(d) Civil and Commercial:
(i) Such originated from private commercial and civil lawsuits that are not segregated to any other court, including leasing and collusion.
(ii) Any civil action submitted against the President of Ecuador. Here, the law provides for the resolution of first instance and appellation. Therefore, there should be no cassation to be admitted against these actions.

(e) Labor:
(i) Such originated from labor relationship lawsuits ruled by the provincial courts.

(f) Family and juvenile:
(i) Such originated from family issues and children issues (including marital status, filiation, matrimony, concubinage, guardianships, and interdictions, and juvenile criminal offenses that are not entrusted to any other court.

§2. VENUE (TERRITORIAL JURISDICTION)

I. Preferred Jurisdiction

29. The venue in which the defendant is to be served process is relevant. In principle, the defendant's personal venue shall be preferred, § 9 COGEP. If the defendant is domiciled in two different venues, either one is an acceptable jurisdiction unless the matter of the litis is related to just one of them. The defendant having no known domicile can be summoned wherever the defendant is found or even through the media (a Major News Paper). Moral persons or legal entities can be served at their registered domicile, principal place of business, or at any of its branches, agencies, or offices. In commercial relationships, the personal venue can be waived, and a different venue can be established by commercial contract (not applicable to employment agreements where only the employees' domicile is the valid venue).

II. Alternative Jurisdiction

30. As mentioned, in principle, a defendant can only be served in the venue corresponding to his/her residency or domicile. However, the defendant can also be served in the following venues:

(i) Wherever the obligation is to be performed or enforced. In Spanish, it is called "payment"; payment is doing what is due. The legal definition of payment in

Ecuador is complying with one's duties (active duties, to do, or passive duties, not to do). Giving, doing, or not doing, that is payment.

(ii) The place of execution of the agreement if at the time of servicing process, the defendant (including through the defendant's general attorney at law) is present in such venue.

(iii) The place at which the defendant has expressly convened to be served through agreement.

(iv) The venue in which the real estate property, matter of the litis, is located.

(v) The place in which losses and damages are caused, including environmental damages.

(vi) The place in which the goods are used or managed, should the matter of the litis concern such goods.

(vii) And the venue applicable to the plaintiff purported alimony claims or claims against the State and its diverse government agencies.

III. Exclusive Jurisdiction

31. There is exclusive jurisdiction in the following circumstances:

(i) in employment relationships, the employee's venue;

(ii) whenever an *in situ* inspection of the subject matter of the litis is required, the venue where the subject matter is located;

(iii) the last domicile of the *de cujus*;

(iv) wherever the succession or inheritance is opened; and

(v) in guardianships, the venue of the guarded individual.

A. Factors to Be Taken into Account

32. All individuals, Ecuadorian or Alien, or any corporation duly incorporated or domiciled in Ecuador, is entitled of being served process according to the Ecuadorian legal provisions. Likewise, any individual, Ecuadorian or Alien, or any corporation duly incorporated or domiciled abroad, is entitled to be served process according to the laws of their corresponding place of domicile. However, Ecuadorian individuals duly registered with an Ecuadorian Consulate may be served process by summoning the individual at the corresponding Ecuadorian Consulate.

B. Main Claims and Ancillary Claims

33. Regarding the jurisdiction in which the real estate property, matter of the litis, is located, when the property is in two or more Counties, the claim should be filed in the jurisdiction where the largest portion lies, or where the property house is located.

The main claim venue is the venue for any other claim.

§3. Resolution of Jurisdiction Conflicts

34. At an administrative level (government agencies), which is the genesis of an administrative process, as the applications serve as claims in these kinds of processes, the jurisdiction conflicts are decided by any higher authority or the Court of Administrative Appeals.

At a judicial level, a Judge may plainly reject a claim based on lacking jurisdiction and return the writ of claim to the plaintiff (this rejecting motion is appealable). Such Judge may also decline jurisdiction and send the process over to the corresponding judge holding jurisdictional. On the other hand, a Judge may also claim jurisdiction and exhort the Judge holding the process but lacks jurisdiction to send the process over. Should there be a jurisdictional conflict at First Instance level where both Judges claim jurisdiction, the conflict will be settled by the Provincial Court. At a Provincial Court level, the conflict shall be ruled by the National Court.

Chapter 2. International Jurisdiction

35. Cross-border matters are subject to conflicts of laws. All American countries, except Canada) signed the International Treaty of Conflicts of Laws so gracefully called Code Sánchez de Bustamante. The U.S.'s Congress did not ratify the Agreement. Through Ecuador's perspective, this means that the Code Sánchez de Bustamante is still applicable in Ecuador to U.S. and Canadian nationals (and any foreigner) but expect not being applicable in the U.S. or Canada to Ecuadorian nationals. Accordingly, some situations should be solved according to *lex fori,* and some situations should be solved according to *lex loci.* Nationality, for instance, shall always be ruled according to lex loci, but certain rights, such as legal age, shall always be ruled pursuant to *lex fori.*

Foreign rulings are executable or enforceable in Ecuador. Former Code of Civil Procedures, abrogated in 2015, entitled the executing judges to review the foreign process in its entirety to validate whether there are no violations to any Ecuadorian legal provision of public order. This was construed as the Ecuadorian Courts being entitled to review the foreign process' merits of the litis. There is no exact definition of provisions of public order really, so the construction was entirely up to the judge. Hence, current COGEP establishes that, provided there are a homologation and exequatur, all foreign rulings are to be executed in Ecuador. Ecuadorian courts have no right to review the merit of the litis now.

This execution of foreign rulings, though, as in any international issues, is subject to reciprocity.

§1. Rules Applicable in the Absence of a Treaty

36. Whenever no international treaty is applicable, the *lex fori*, that is Ecuadorian law, would apply.

§2. International Treaties

37. First, it is important to know that international treaties in Ecuador are higher in the hierarchy to Congress Acts, § 424 of the Constitution. The Constitution is the highest provision, and the international treaties are just under. There are really no bilateral treaties regarding civil procedures, but there are plenty of applicable multilateral treaties. One of the most relevant multilateral treaties is the treaty of conflicts of laws or international private law gracefully called Code "Sánchez de Bustamante." This is basically a treaty applicable to all American countries, except for Canada that did not sign it and the United States of America who did sign it but did not ratify it in the U.S. Congress.

Anyhow, there are those who believe that multilateral treaties are equally applicable, obviously not by the non-member countries but against them as well. Therefore, in Ecuador, the Code Sánchez de Bustamante might be equally applicable against the U.S. and Canada, and even any non-American country. However arguable, it seems to gain favorability by current Justices.

Part III. Actions and Claims

38. It is difficult to identify the difference between actions versus claims. A "*pretensión*" literally translated into English as a pretension, would be the volition of a person, what that person pretends or wants, what that person considers or believes it is appropriate, correct, just, and righteous. Rights are such pretensions or volitions legally or juridically protected, protected by law, or duly entitled. The claim would be the right to request the courts the recognition of such entitlements and to rule accordingly. And action would be the exercising of such claim.

Despite that, there are those who would rather consider claim as the exercising of such rights, and action as the exercise of such right of claim.

Chapter 1. Actions

§1. Definition

39. COGEP does not define or provide a concept for action or the right of action; it might be defined as the act of filing a claim or the right to request the courts to rule on a certain matter.

§2. Admissibility

40. In Ecuador, the right of action, that is the right to file a claim should be unquestionable. In other words, the courts should always accept all actions whatsoever, so that within the process, the plaintiff is entitled to elaborate the evidence given the opportunity to prove the validity of its claim. That was the essence of the former Code of Civil Procedures. Presumably, the courts were inundated with procedural cases, so now judges are entitled to dismiss a claim when they consider that it is not substantiated enough or vexatious. For instance, if wanted to claim rights of property over the moon, most probably the claim will be rejected, hence forfeiting the plaintiff the right to submit the corresponding evidence if any.

§3. Vexatious Litigation

41. Current COGEP provides for the rejection of vexatious litigation; however, such prerogative may leave honest litigants undefended. Vexatious litigation should be punished but not rejected. Anyhow, in Ecuador, vexatious litigation, in addition to being punishable by the Antitrust Act, may also be rejected before being accepted to process.

Chapter 2. Claims and Defenses

42. As mentioned, a claim would be the exercise of the right of action, which is the right to request the courts to rule whether a volition or pretension is juridically protected or not. The defense would be the answer to that claim, provided the claim has been submitted against a particular person. In voluntary jurisdiction, there is no legitimate contradictor or defendant.

§1. Definition

43. If action is the right to file a claim requesting the courts the recognition of a pretension that the plaintiff believes being entitled to and to rule accordingly, the defense would be the right to answer to that claim requesting the courts the rejection of the plaintiff's pretensions that the defendant considers the plaintiff is not entitled to, and to rule accordingly.

§2. Distinctions (Main Claims, Ancillary Claims; Defense on the Merits and Procedural "Exceptions")

44. If by ancillary we mean subsidiary, supplementary, or secondary, no ancillary claims are permissible in Ecuador. The court should reject all ancillary claims in that respect. However, if by ancillary we mean an additional claim having connectivity over the main claim (such as principal and interests), then such claims can well be accumulated or submitted in the same writ of claim.

Only the following are permissible prior exceptions, § 153 COGEP:

1. lack of jurisdiction of the court, §13 COGEP;
2. incapacity or lack of personality of the plaintiff or his/her representative (lack of personality is that the person is not who such person claims to be), §31 COGEP;
3. lack of legitimacy of the process or incomplete conformation of *litis consortium*;
4. error in the way the claim was proposed, incorrect proceeding, or undue accumulation of pretensions;
5. *litispendencia* (exact same claim being processed at another court);
6. applicability of the Statute of Limitations (some rights are subject to a statute of limitations);
7. expiration (some actions are subject to expiration);
8. *res judicata*;
9. settlement; and
10. mediation or arbitration agreement.

Even though, civil procedures are considered to be verbal, and the defense is to be submitted orally at a public hearing, the exceptions are to be submitted in a written format within thirty days after being summoned.

Most answers, unless expressly banned, are entitled to include a counterclaim, for which the plaintiff will be granted a three days' period (as opposed to the thirty days granted to the defendant) to answer the counterclaim.

Chapter 3. Sanctions on Procedural Irregularities

45. If the irregularity does not seriously affect the process or minor irregularities (i.e., not appearing at a certain audience requesting date and time for another audience; not rising when the judges or Justices enter the court venue), there would be no major consequences; if the irregularity may affect the process, the infringer may be called his attention; if the irregularity does affect the process, the infringer will be imposed a pecuniary sanction, disbarred, or even criminally prosecuted.

§1. Formal Requirements

46. All formal requirements must be submitted in writing. The litigating parties may only meet the judge or Justices with its counterpart presence. Colloquial contacts with the clerks are not considered irregular though.

§2. Time Limits

47. The law provides for certain time limits that the court must obey; however, most time limits must be officially and expressly granted by the court.

Part IV. Proceedings

Chapter 1. Pretrial Proceedings (If Any)

48. The law provides for exemplary acceptable pretrial proceedings or preparatory measures but not limitative, § 122 COGEP such as:

(i) Exhibition of movable goods that are to be sequestered or seized.
(ii) Exhibition of a deed of transfer of property.
(iii) The acknowledgment of a signature affixed to a private document.
(iv) The appointment of a guardian.
(v) The opening of safety deposit boxes from the institutions of the financial system (i.e., banks).
(vi) The preparatory inspection if the matter of the litis can be altered or lost.

Chapter 2. Proceedings in First Instance

49. The new Code of Civil Procedures provides for the following procedures:

(i) Ordinary.
(ii) Summary.
(iii) Executive.
(iv) *Monitorio*.
(v) Voluntary.

All of which, except for the voluntary proceeding, are contentious or adversary proceedings.

§1. Adversary Proceedings

I. Ordinary Proceedings

A. Introduction of the Claim

50. Pursuant to § 141 of COGEP, every process starts with the filing of a claim but can be preceded by the corresponding pretrial proceedings. This article, though, is incorrect, for the same Code provides that voluntary proceedings are initiated with the filing of an application (not a claim). Claims and applications, by definition, are not the same. Anyhow, both the claim and the application must be submitted in writing and shall contain:

(i) the identification of the subject matter, competent jurisdictional judge, and venue;
(ii) plaintiff's complete names (given names, first, middle and third name if any, surname, and mother's maiden surname), I.D. No., marital status, age, profession or way of living, domicile, address, e-mail address, judicial domicile (attorney at law's judicial box, or e-mail judicial box); the same identity information is applicable to the attorney at law;
(iii) Tax. I.D. where applicable;
(iv) complete names and domicile of the defendant (including e-mail if available);
(v) complete matter of facts as precise, summarized and edited as possible;
(vi) the applicable legal provisions;
(vii) the evidence that shall be submitted (including the names of the witnesses and the facts that they shall narrate), and the things that shall be considered a matter of the litis (*in situ* inspections, expert reports);
(viii) the request for the exhibition of documents if pertinent;
(ix) the value of the claim or amount that is being claimed;
(x) the type of proceeding that is to take place (i.e., ordinary, executive, special, *monitorio* or voluntary); and
(xi) the signature of plaintiff and attorney at law.

1. Notice (Service, Including Service Abroad, Etc.)

51. Summons is the act by which a defendant is made known with the tenor of a claim or petition of a pretrial proceeding that has been initiated, and the motions that affect them, ensuring the right of the defendant to submit answers and counter evidence. Summons must be accomplished by a registered and licensed bailiff and according to Ecuadorian legal provisions, even if the defendant is foreign and the proceeding is initiated abroad.

Once the judge of first instance has accepted a claim as coherent, valid, and complete, the court shall send a motion to the Summons Office so that a bailiff may proceed with serving the defendant process to: (i) Ecuadorian citizens domiciled in Ecuador and foreign individuals domiciled in Ecuador; and (ii) Ecuadorian companies and foreign companies domiciled in Ecuador. If the defendant is abroad, the judge should send the motion (Summons or Letters Rogatory) to the corresponding Ecuadorian Consul to continue with the applicable summons proceeding as follows:

(i) The defendant is an Ecuadorian citizen domiciled abroad:
- (a) If the defendant has registered his/her domicile in any Ecuadorian Consulate, the Consul shall place the summons in the Consulate's cardboard for three consecutive days.
- (b) If the defendant has not registered his/her domicile in any Ecuadorian Consulate, the Consul shall send the Letters Rogatory to the Supreme Court of the host country for serving the defendant according to the laws of the host country. However, it has been misconstrued this provision to the point that Ecuadorian Consuls have managed to interact as bailiffs trying to serve the defendants, and even sending the summons by Courier for three consecutive times.

(ii) The defendant is a foreign citizen domiciled abroad.

In this case, the Consul should send the Letters Rogatory to the Supreme Court of the host country for serving the defendant according to the laws of the host country.

(iii) The defendant is a foreign moral entity (company).

In this case, the Consul should send the Letters Rogatory to the Supreme Court of the host country for serving the defendant according to the laws of the host country.

2. Registration by the Court

52. Any writ submitted to the courts by the defendant in each case will be considered as a waiver of the summons and shall be held as served. In other words, in any case that the defendant claims not having been served process validly, the defendant shall be considered summoned at the time the defendant appears in court.

3. Summary Judgment (If Any)

53. At the judgment hearing, the judge shall render his/her verdict but may take the corresponding time to issue the duly grounded ruling in writing.

B. Progress of Proceedings

1. Preparatory Measures (Including Production of Documents, Exchange of Pleadings)

54. The law provides for exemplary acceptable pretrial proceedings or preparatory measures, but it is not limitative, such as:

(i) Exhibition of movable goods that are to be sequestered or seized.
(ii) Exhibition of the deed of transfer of property.
(iii) The recognition of the signing of a private document.
(iv) The appointment of guardian.
(v) The opening of safety boxes from the institutions of the financial system (i.e., banks).
(vi) The preparatory inspection if the matter of the litis can be altered or lost.

2. Purely Written Procedure (If Any)

55. Labor and family proceedings were transformed into oral proceedings in order to allow the lawyers to get used to the orality. However, these two types of proceedings, although they can be oral, even now, can be entirely written proceedings.

3. Determination of the Trial Date

56. Once the defendant has been duly served process (validly or not); the defendant will have a certain period of time, depending on the process, to submit his/her answers, and three days after such period expires (or the term to submit answers to the counterclaim), the judge shall set a date and time for the first preliminary hearing:

(i) Ordinary proceedings:
   (a) thirty business days to submit answers to the main claim;
   (b) three business days to answer any counterclaim; and
   (c) three days for scheduling the preliminary hearing, which must be neither lower than ten days nor higher than twenty days. Should there be no additional evidence to consider, judgment can be issued in this preliminary hearing.

(ii) Summary Proceedings:
  (a) Fifteen business days to submit answers to the main claim.
  (b) Within thirty business days after the defendant has submitted answers.
  (c) There is only one hearing in which ruling shall be issued.

(iii) Executive proceedings:
  (a) fifteen business days to submit answers to the main claim;
  (b) fifteen business days to answer any counterclaim submitted with another executive security;
  (c) should there be no payment or answer within the corresponding term, the judge shall issue its judgment right away (there are no recourses over this judgment);
  (d) a single hearing shall be scheduled within twenty days after the defendant has submitted its answer; and
  (e) this proceeding is subject to appeal but not to cassation.

(iv) *Monitorio* (up to USD 20,000):
  (a) fifteen business days to submit answers to the main claim (no counterclaim allowed);
  (b) should there be no payment or answer within the corresponding term, the judge shall issue its judgment right away (there are no recourses over this judgment);
  (c) the single hearing shall be scheduled within twenty days after the defendant has submitted its answer; and
  (d) this proceeding is subject to appeal but not to cassation.

(v) Voluntary proceedings:
  (a) Within ten to thirty days after summoning all interested parties if ever, the judge shall call for a single and definite hearing. Any opposition will convert the voluntary proceeding into an adversary proceeding following the structure of a summary proceeding.

4. Trial (Including Representation of Parties, Examination by the Trial Judge, Adjournment, Etc.)

57. Once a claim is submitted, the judge if needed, shall examine the claim and request the plaintiff to clarify or complete the claim. Once the claim is considered clear and complete, the judge shall summon the defendant; once the defendant has been served process, the judge will request the defendant to submit its answers; if no answers are submitted, it shall be considered a plain rejection of all merits of the claim.

Then, the judge shall call for a preliminary hearing in which all possible evidence shall be evacuated or pondered, and if no additional evidence is to be considered *post event*, the judge shall issue his/her verdict. Once the verdict is issued, the parties are entitled to appeal. All these events are to take place orally. If the judge needs time to further evaluate his/her decision (on an extraordinary basis), the judge may take ten days for rendering his/her oral judgment. The judge may take an additional ten days for writing down his/her sentence.

Should there be additional evidence to consider post event (i.e., judicial inspections, submission of counterpart documents, etc.), the judge shall evacuate or proceed with such evidence and call for a judgment hearing for the parties to render their closing arguments, in which the verdict shall be issued. Again, if the judge needs time to evaluate or write down his/her verdict, the judge shall take some time to that effect.

If for any reason whatsoever, the defeated party did not appeal in the judgment hearing, the right to appeal shall preclude, having no other chance to appeal.

5. Opinion by the *"Ministère Public"* (If Any)

58. In Ecuador, there is no *Ministère public* considered as an authority in charge of defending the interests of the people and due application of law in every process. However, there is the *Ombudsman* who is an officer in charge of representing the interests of the people in their particular claims of public interest.

C. Judgment

1. Deliberation

59. Once the parties have rendered their closing arguments, the judge shall issue his/her oral verdict orally. The oral verdict can be adjourned on an extraordinary basis when the merits of the claim make the adjournment indefectible. The oral ruling does not have to be well substantiated; the substantiation of the judgment shall be rendered in a written form.

2. Different Kinds of Judgments

60. There are no different kinds of judgments; every case will have its own particular judgment, though. But there are three types of judicial pronunciations:

(a) Substantiation Auto.—Is the judicial motion by which the judge orders the continuity of the process (i.e., Appointment of experts).
(b) Interlocutory Auto.—Is the judicial motion by which the judge decides on procedural issues, which, even though are not a part of the main claim, are essential in the administration of justice (i.e., rejection of writ of claim).
(c) Sentence or Judgment.—Is the judicial motion by which the judge decides on an irrevocable basis on the merits of the claim.

3. Formal Aspects of the Judgment

61. All written rulings shall be well reasoned; otherwise, they are to be considered null and void. It will be considered that there is no such reasoning if: (i) within the main body of the judgment there are no references to the legal provisions, juridical principles, or judicial precedents in which the judgment is grounded or cemented; and (ii) it is not explained why such laws, principles, and precedents are pertinent with respect to the facts. The voidance of the judgment can only be used as part of an appeal or Cassation Recourse.

All Autos or Judgments shall have: (i) the identification of the judge; (ii) date and time; (iii) the identification of plaintiff, defendant, and third parties if any; (iv) the factual recitals; (v) the reasoning; (vi) the precise decision; and (vii) the judge's signature.

Oral Judgments shall contain: (i) a clear and precise exposition of the merits of the case; (ii) the specification of the thing, the quantity, or the fact that is being accepted or rejected; and (iii) if there is merit for collecting damages, interests, and expenses.

Written judgments shall contain: (i) the identification of the judge; (ii) date and time; (iii) the identification of plaintiff, defendant, and third parties if any; (iv) a brief enunciation of the facts and circumstances that are the merit of the claim and the defendant's answers or defense; (v) an express resolution over each answer; (vi) an essay over the proven facts that are relevant to the resolution; (vii) the reasoning; (viii) the resolution on the merits of the claim, specifying the thing, the quantity, or the fact to which the defendant is punished if any; and (ix) should there be merits for charging damages, interests, or expenses. In addition, if any of the parties belong to a *Kichua* or *Shuar* nationality, the ruling must be translated into any such language.

4. Notice and Service

62. The judgment shall be considered noticed at the time the judgment is rendered orally at the judgment hearing.

5. Res Judicata

63. Res judicata must be called by the defendant as an exception in the defendant's answers. The court is not entitled to rule res judicata ex officio.

6. Interpretation and Rectification of Judgments

64. At the hearing, once the judgment has been noticed, both litigants may submit a Clarification and Amplification Recourse, or within three days after the judgment has been handed down (if after a hearing). An appeal or the Cassation recourse may only be submitted after the Clarification and Amplification Recourse has been absolved or replied by the court.

The Judgment can be amplified if it did not cover all the claims, but it cannot be revoked or rectified by any circumstance. Not even if the Judgment is wrong.

7. Penalty in Case of Non-compliance (If Available)

65. Should the plaintiff have initiated provisional proceedings, the court shall order the custodian, the debtor, or the Real Estate Property, Maritime, or Aircraft Registrar, to proceed according to the ruling. Otherwise, the court will order the seizure of any goods that may cover the ruling amount. Non-compliance with a Court order is subject to criminal charges. If the debtor is not able to pay, a bankruptcy or insolvency proceeding shall be initiated.

II. Provisional Proceedings

66. Prior to submitting a claim, the plaintiff may request the following measures to secure goods:

(i) Seizure of tangible movables—Should there be a reasonable belief that the defendant has no further means to cover the Judgment in case of success, and that the tangible goods matter of the litis may disappear (transferred or hidden away); the plaintiff may request the seizing of such goods so as to be handed in custody to an official custodian.

(ii) Withholding of intangible movables (debts, rights, or entitlements)—The plaintiff may request that the debtor retains or withholds repayments so that in case the process is overcome by the plaintiff, the claim is honored by such debtor.

(iii) Transfer Ban—The way to seize immovables (including vessels and aircrafts, which, even though are movables, are considered immovables for legal purposes) is by prohibiting the Real Estate Property, and Maritime or Aircraft Registrars to refrain from recording any transfer of property over the immovables, vessels or aircrafts matter of the litis.

§2. Default Proceedings

67. Default proceedings —The proceedings in which one or more defendants fail to submit a timely answer shall takc its course. The judge will consider ex officio that the surrendering defendant has submitted a plain and simple negative, rejection or challenge to all and every claim. For continuing with a default proceeding, all known and identified defendants must have been duly served.

§3. Ex Parte Proceedings

68. Ex parte proceedings, in principle, are not valid in Ecuador. As being duly served is an essential part of due process, lack of summoning would revert into the nullity of the process. However, as soon as the defendant appears to the court, the process becomes an Adversary Proceeding. Yet, for the lack of summoning to invalidate the process, the defendant must be deprived of the right to submit answers and evidence.

On the other hand, should the defendant be impossible to find, the defendant can be summoned by a publication in a major newspaper; in which case, the judge will consider a plain and simple rejection to all claims by the defendant. Perhaps, this may be considered as the one valid ex parte proceeding.

Ex parte proceedings that are conducted for the benefit of only one party, where there is no adversary are called Voluntary Jurisdiction Proceedings. Whenever a third party challenges the voluntary proceeding, it becomes an Adversary Proceeding.

§4. Voluntary Proceedings

69. Voluntary Jurisdiction Proceedings are subject to their own and swifter proceeding. This proceeding is such that it is not intended to be contested or challenged as they are for the benefit of the plaintiff's only (such as the acquisition of property by means of the statute of limitations, or granting rights to a minor that has not been emancipated). However, whenever the Voluntary Jurisdiction Proceeding is contested or challenged, the proceeding reverts into an Adversary Proceeding, subject to the proceedings and regulation of any litigious proceeding.

Chapter 3. Review Proceedings

§1. Appeal

70. Some proceedings are subject to appeal before the Provincial or Appellate Court. The appeal must be claimed at the Judgment hearing at the time the ruling is being verbalized; otherwise, it will be considered extemporaneous. At this instance, only new evidence (evidence that was not available before) may be submitted.

In Ecuador, once there is a final judgment, lawyers can file a claim against their clients for delinquent legal fees, which shall be solved by the same First Instance Judge as an incident of the main claim. The first instance ruling on legal fees that will most probably favor the lawyer is final and is not susceptible of any legal recourse (Appeal, Cassation, or Constitutional) arguably prompting lawyers and judges to the worst-case scenarios.

§2. Cassation (If Any)

71. There is indeed Cassation in Ecuador. It is not considered an appeal or third instance, but a separate recourse submitted against illegal rulings from the Provincial or Appellate Court. In other words, the Supreme or National Court should not reevaluate the evidence or the merits of the process; it should only rectify any wrongdoing, misconstruction of the law, or wrongful disregard of duties in the application of the law. The Court *ad quem* may overturn the ruling *a quo*, though, if needed.

§3. Extraordinary Appeals

72. There is no third instance or extraordinary appeals in Ecuador. The cassation recourse is not considered an appeal but a separate proceeding. However, there is an extraordinary lawsuit before the Constitutional Court which can be submitted against unconstitutional rulings from the National Court.

Part V. Incidents

§1. Withdrawal and Discontinuance of Action

73. The claim can be withdrawn, and the parties may settle their differences at any time prior to the pronunciation of the final judgment. And the process shall be considered abandoned or discontinued, in either first or second instances, or at cassation, when all the parties have ceased from prosecuting for six months, counted from the date of notice of the last useful motion. No abandonment is considered when it is up to the court to continue the process.

§2. Challenge of Judges

74. The judges may be challenged for the following reasons:

(i) Being part of the process as plaintiff, defendant, witness, or having any type of interest in the process.
(ii) Being the spouse or concubine of any party to the process or their defendants.
(iii) Being close relative to any party to the process or their legal representative, agent, defendants or the judge *a quo*.
(iv) Having ruled in another instance and in the same process or any connected matter, or having acted as mediator.
(v) Lack of excuse for delaying its judicial activity.
(vi) Having been legal representative, agent, defendant, of any party to the process.
(vii) Having granted advise or opinion over the process.
(viii) Having any conflict with any of the parties to the process.
(ix) Having received any rights, contributions, goods, securities, monies, or services.
(x) Having any party to the process or their defendants pending obligations.
(xi) Having any party to the process or their defendants intimate or close friendship or enmity.
(xii) Having a personal interest in the process, due to personal business or that of his/her spouse or concubine, or close relatives.

Part VI. Legal Aid and Legal Costs

Chapter 1. Legal Aid

75. There are several gratuitous legal aids at certain Centers, such as the ones formed by universities and certain foundations. Since these are private entities, virtually anyone can apply for gratuitous legal aid; however, for obvious reasons, the Centers will make sure that the applicant does not have enough means to procure a paid attorney at law.

Chapter 2. Legal Costs

76. Arbitration proceedings' costs depend on the arbitration venue. Although there was a time when judicial proceedings were charged a fee, currently, judicial proceedings are free of judicial costs; some proceedings do not even require the assistance of a lawyer. The defeated litigant may be charged to pay attorney's fees and costs, but usually are irrelevant to take into consideration.

Part VII. Evidence

Chapter 1. Burden of Proof

77. The burden of proof is always burdened on the one that makes an allegation. All allegations must be proven; yet, plain negatives, contradictions, oppositions or rejections are not burdened with the burden of proof.

Chapter 2. Admissibility of Evidence

78. Whenever the evidence has been submitted in an orderly fashion, that is, having been announced at the time of filing the claim or when submitting the answers and disclosed or performed at the preliminary hearing, the evidence should be admitted in court. Otherwise, the evidence should be rejected.

If the defendant has submitted evidence or new arguments that must be reargued, the plaintiff will be granted the right to announce new evidence that shall be disclosed or performed at the preliminary audience.

A new development with the new Code of Civil Procedures is that in certain circumstances, new unannounced evidence can be submitted even up at the Provincial Court level, provided such evidence was not available or could not be obtained when due.

Chapter 3. Administration of Evidence

§1. Forced Production of Documents

79. The court could subpoena the parties ex officio or at the parties' request to produce documents. This will be performed at the preliminary hearing; or if needed, the court will set a day and time to that effect.

§2. Deposition by Witnesses

80. All third parties' depositions must be anticipated or announced in the writ of claim or the writ of answers. The witnesses shall be subpoenaed accordingly and called to appear in court at the preliminary hearing in which the parties (represented by their lawyers) shall verbally inquire the witnesses, and the witnesses shall render their testimony accordingly.

A deposition cannot take place out of court unless the circumstances require that the judge travels to wherever the witnesses reside or that the testimony be rendered via videoconference; however, in no case, the deposition can be rendered without a judge present. Depositions cannot take place before a Notary Public, and cannot be rendered in advance unless there is a pretrial process to that effect. An affidavit, on the other hand, can be executed in advance, though, but it would not be a deposition.

§3. Deposition by the Parties Themselves

81. The parties can request the court to hear their testimony or request the court to hear their counterpart's testimony. These self-depositions must be anticipated in the writ of claim or in the answers. At the preliminary hearing, the parties shall be heard and may be questioned by their counterparts.

Such depositions, though, cannot take place out of court unless the circumstances require that the judge travels to wherever the party rendering testimony resides or that the deposition be rendered via videoconference; however, in no case, the confession can be rendered without a judge present; it cannot take place before a Notary Public and cannot be rendered in advance unless there is a pretrial process to that effect. An affidavit can be executed in advance, though, but not a confession.

§4. Expert Evidence

82. Only official experts duly registered with the Judiciary Council can be enlisted. Such experts shall be enlisted by the plaintiff and by the defendant so that the claim and answers can be submitted along with the expertise report. If both plaintiff and defendant have submitted equivocal expertise reports, the court shall appoint a third expert from the registered official experts, whose expertise report shall be final. The judge is not forced to accept the considerations of any expertise report.

§5. Affidavit

83. Notarial or judicial affidavits are equally applicable and acceptable. Voluntary depositions before a Notary Public or a judge are called affidavits; but, in an adversary proceeding, the institution is called "testimony."

§6. Inspection by the Judge

84. Judges are entitled and prompted to perform personal *in situ* inspections in order to verify the goods' status, location, and maintenance when such goods cannot be transported to the court's venue, either because they are immovable, adhered to a real estate property, or are too big to be transported to the judge's venue.

Part VIII. Seizure for Security and Enforcement of Judgments

Chapter 1. Seizure for Security

§1. Proceedings

85. Prior to submitting a claim, the plaintiff may request the following measures to secure goods:

(i) Seizure of tangible movables. Should there be a reasonable belief that the defendant has no further means to cover the sentence in case of success, and that the tangible goods matter of the litis may disappear (transferred or hidden away); the plaintiff may request seizing such goods so as to be handed in custody to an official custodian.
(ii) Withholding of intangible movables (debts, rights, or entitlements). The plaintiff may request that the debtor retains or withholds repayments so that in case the process is overcome by the plaintiff, the claim is honored by such debtor.
(iii) Transfer Ban. The way to seize immovables (including vessels and aircrafts; which, even though are movables, are considered immovables for legal purposes) is by prohibiting the Real Estate Property, and Maritime, and or the Aircraft Registrars to refrain from recording any transfer of property over the immovable, vessels or aircrafts matter of the litis.

§2. Judicial Review

86. Some judicial motions can be reviewed by a higher court and subject to judicial review by the Provincial Court, or the National Court (if illegal).

Chapter 2. Enforcement of Judgments

87. The First Instance Judge, once there is a final or enforceable judgment after all recourses have been processed, is entitled and bound to enforce the final ruling if favoring the plaintiff. The Judge will send motions to all registrars for seizing the corresponding goods. It will send motions to all banks in which the defendant has deposits, and to all debtors to the defendant so as to seize the defendant's credits. The proceeding will be like the proceeding for Seizure for Security.

§1. Enforcement of Domestic Judgments

I. Proceedings

88. The Judge of first instance oversees enforcing the ruling, either by receiving payment from the defendant or seizing the corresponding goods.

II. Judicial Review

89. No judicial review is applicable unless the judge is abusing his/her authority, in which case, there are legal actions to halt any illegality.

§2. Recognition and Enforcement of Foreign Judgments

90. All duly homologated foreign judgments and settlements are enforceable in Ecuador. The Ecuadorian courts are not entitled to review the merits of the process or should they contravene any Ecuadorian legal provision of public order. The law is silent with respect to arbitration awards; however, by way of recognizing the validity of foreign judgments and mediation minutes, it should be implied that foreign arbitration awards should also be recognized in Ecuador. Anyhow, this recognition is subject to reciprocity.

I. Rules Applicable in the Absence of a Treaty

91. The corresponding specialized court of the Provincial Court shall have jurisdiction over the recognition and homologation of international rulings and mediation minutes with judgment force in their country of origin, for which the following is required:

(i) That the ruling has all the external formalities required for being considered authentic in its country of origin.
(ii) That the ruling is considered res judicata in its country of origin and that the annexed documentation has been duly legalized.
(iii) Duly translated into Spanish if in another language.

(iv) The defendant must have been duly summoned or served and that the parties due process has been secured (the law mentions the word "*notificada,*" which is Spanish for "notice"; it should say "*citada*" which is the Spanish for being served process. Hence, it is not clear whether the homologation requires that the defendant has been duly served process, or that the former has been duly noticed with the judgment.

(v) That the application for homologation of ruling provides for the exact address of the defendant against the ruling shall be executed.

For homologating a foreign judgment, the plaintiff shall submit an application to the corresponding Provincial Court who, after reviewing the above requirements, shall send summons the defendant at his/her given address. Once duly served, the defendant shall have five days to file an opposition to the homologation, and the judge shall have thirty days from the date of summons to rule over the homologation. Should there be merits for a hearing, the court shall call for one in which the homologation shall be ruled. There is no recourse applicable to this ruling (except for clarification and explanation purposes).

Once homologated, the foreign judgment shall be good for execution. The execution of foreign judgments corresponds to the judge of first instance of the defendant's domicile. If the defendant does not have a domicile in Ecuador, the jurisdiction corresponds to the domicile in which the goods matter of the litis are held or located.

Any foreign ruling that is to be used in Ecuador for evidentiary purposes must be homologated.

II. International Treaties

92. The law provides that duly homologated foreign rulings and mediation minutes that were handed down in adversary or non-adversary proceedings shall have in Ecuador the legal force as provided for by enforceable international treaties, not being applicable to any review of the merits of the foreign process. In addition to that, the law provides that duly enforceable international treaties have prevalence over Congress Acts.

International Treaties:

- United Nations Conventions on the Recognition and Enforcement of Foreign Judgments in Civil and Commercial Matters, concluded on February 1, 1971.
- United Nations Convention on the Service Abroad of Judicial and Extrajudicial Documents in Civil or Commercial Matters, concluded on November 15, 1965.
- Inter/American Convention on Letters Rogatory of January 1, 1975.

Part IX. Arbitration

93. Arbitration is an applicable alternative method to make justice in Ecuador. There is no appeal or cassation to arbitration awards, but a nullity action can be tried at the Provincial Court (with cassation recourse).

Chapter 1. Arbitrability

94. Only cases that can be settled can be submitted to arbitration. For instance, labor conflicts are not subject to arbitration, as in strict sense no settlement is applicable in labor relationships, as labor rights cannot be waived, and thus not subject to settlement.

Chapter 2. Arbitration Agreement and Party Autonomy

95. The arbitration agreement must be expressed and in writing. The parties are free from establishing their own arbitration proceeding in matters that are not expressly prohibited by law.

Chapter 3. Composition of Arbitral Tribunal

96. The parties are free to establish the composition of the arbitral tribunal. However, if the case is to be awarded in law (and not in equity), the arbitrators must be duly admitted attorneys at law. Whenever the composition of the arbitral tribunal has not been considered by the parties, the rules of the arbitration center and the Arbitration and Mediation Act shall apply.

Chapter 4. Conduct of Arbitral Proceedings

97. The proceeding must be conducted in Spanish unless it is an international arbitration with the venue in Ecuador.

Chapter 5. Arbitral Award

98. The arbitral award must be handed down within 150 days counted from the date of the substantiation hearing, but it can be extended for another 150 days, if the parties agree to, or the tribunal considers necessary.

Chapter 6. Recourse Against Arbitral Award

99. There is no recourse (Appel or Cassation) against the arbitral awards, except for the nullity recourse which shall be submitted before the Chief Justice of the Provincial or Appellate Court. The causes of nullity are:

(a) when the defendant has not been duly served process, and the proceeding has been processed ex parte;
(b) when the motions have not been duly noticed to any of the parties;
(c) when no evidentiary hearing has been accomplished, should there were evidence to be submitted;
(d) *extra petita* or *plus petita*; or,
(e) when the legal proceedings have been violated.

Chapter 7. Recognition and Enforcement of Awards

100. Should the award be not immediately honored by the defendant, the arbitrators may request the assistance of the public force, or the plaintiff may request the ordinary courts to execute the award. The latter is usual.

Chapter 8. International Arbitration

101. By principle, international arbitration agreements are legally binding should the parties, at the time of signing the arbitration agreement, are domiciled in two separate States. No international arbitration is valid should both parties reside in Ecuador; unless: (i) a substantial part of a contract is to be performed abroad or the matter of the litis is located abroad; or, (ii) the matter of the litis contemplates an international commercial transaction that is subject to settlement.

Part X. Mediation

102. Should there be no mediation process prior to an adversary proceeding (whether there is a settlement or not); the Judge of first instance may (but is not compulsory) send the process for mediation. Usually, Judges take this opportunity in order to momentarily alleviate their burden of work.

Chapter 1. Legislation/Definitions

103. Mediation is as legally binding as arbitration provided the mediation process ends up in a settlement agreement. A mediation minutes meddling a settlement agreement is as enforceable as an arbitration award, and mediators, as well as arbitrators, have the same judicial capacity and recognition to validate settlement agreements. They are judges on their own right.

Chapter 2. Rights That Can Be Subject to Mediation

104. The same rights that can be subject to arbitration can be subject to mediation; except for labor rights that can also be subject to mediation.

Chapter 3. Mediation Agreement

105. The mediation agreement must be expressed and in writing. Whenever the parties have agreed to mediation, this proceeding must be accomplished prior to any other litigious proceeding, either judicial or arbitral.

On the lack of mediation agreement, any party is free from inviting any other party to a mediation process at any time. The counterpart is free from accepting the invitation, but not forced to reach an agreement; or from rejecting the invitation. Rejecting the invitation, though, may be considered as an act of bad faith; unless, of course, there is an ongoing adversary proceeding.

Chapter 4. Persons/Institutions That Can Act as Mediator

106. The law provides that mediation may be requested to any registered Mediation Centre or any duly authorized independent mediators. However, since accepting a mediation invitation is optional and the mediation if it has a happy ending, ends in a voluntary Transactional Agreement or Undertaking, anyone could act as a mediator, really. On the other hand, though, in order to submit to the courts a Lack-of-Settlement Certificate, only official certificates issued by duly registered Mediation Centers are valid.

Chapter 5. Mediation Procedure

107. Once one party has filed a mediation application, the mediator or the Mediation Centre shall invite the counterpart and call him/her to a mediation hearing. If the counterpart accepts the invitation, the hearing will take place. If the parties reach an agreement, a Mediation Minutes will be drafted and signed by all parties, including the Mediator. Should there be no agreement, the Mediator shall draft a Lack of Agreement Minutes. In case the process has been delivered by the court, the Mediator shall send the process along with the corresponding Minutes to the court.

Chapter 6. Settlement Agreement

108. Should the parties reach a settlement agreement or an undertaking, which could be reached in or out of court, the conflict will be over. If the settlement agreement or undertaking is reached at an Arbitration and Mediation Center, or at court, the agreement shall be validated by the Arbitrator, the Mediator, or the Court, accordingly, and the case will be dismissed. Any conflict resolved by a valid and binding settlement agreement is considered to be res judicata.

Chapter 7. Setting Aside a Settlement Agreement

109. All validly executing and binding agreements are considered lawful; hence, a settlement agreement is final. There are no recourses applicable to the matters duly resolved by a valid settlement agreement, not even nullity recourses. Nullity recourses are applicable to invalid settlement agreements, though.

Chapter 8. International Mediation

110. Since accepting a mediation invitation is optional and considering that the mediation may end in a voluntary settlement agreement or undertaking, anyone could act as mediator; hence, international mediation is perfectly licit. However, in order to submit to the courts a Lack-of-Settlement Certificate, only certificates issued by Ecuadorian Mediation Centers are acceptable.

Selected Bibliography

Constitution of 2008, as amended.
General Proceedings Organic Code of 2015, as amended.
Judicial Organic Code of 2009, as amended.
General Resolutions from the Judiciary Council.
Arbitration and Mediation Act of 2006, as amended.
Civil Code of 2005, as amended.
Commercial Code of 2019, as amended.
Code Sánchez de Bustamante of 1928.

Selected Bibliography

www.ingramcontent.com/pod-product-compliance
Ingram Content Group UK Ltd.
Pitfield, Milton Keynes, MK11 3LW, UK
UKHW020151290926
15471UKWH00004B/802